<u>Dedication</u>

I'd like to dedicate this book to all the ladies that have gone through a break-up—not necessarily a bad one—but a difficult one and not necessarily with a boyfriend, but with a boy "friend"; my mom Oty, my two amazing daughters, Kacee and Violet, my best friends, and, soul mates, Anita, Alexa and Nana, the friends who stayed up helping me get through the editing process, Diana, Ashley and Elizabeth (Eli) and to the boy "friends" who made this possible.

The Fulfiller (Introvert) Virgo
The Visionary (Extrovert) Leo
The Thinker (Introvert) Scorpio
The Executive (Extrovert) Libra
The Protector (Introvert) Gemini

Without the craziness, the lessons, the love, the heartbreaks, the reality, the trials and the tribulations, this would have never been possible. There are some things that don't have a beginning or end, they just continuously and consistently are. Writing is that beginning-less, endless, continuous, consistent thing for me. I can't explain it. Perhaps, I'm not supposed to. Thank you, boys, for giving me a better understanding of me.

But, I'd like to especially dedicate this book to my sister—Sandra—who taught me how to be an "eternal optimist" and who will always be my Wonder Woman.

Introduction

A lot of people ask me why I write and although I find that I am not able to give anyone a logical explanation when I am asked that question my mind does take off. Imagine yourself looking at you from the outside. Imagine being the observer of yourself and seeing your life from another perspective.

That's how I feel. Aside from the fact that I think in perfect portraits, there is also background music to every thought and every moment. This is what makes me want to tell the story.

To enjoy this ride to its fullest I suggest you equip yourself with access to two things: Your imagination and iTunes (or a diverse musical play list of some sort). On occasion, you may see the words "Just press play:" followed by an artist and a song name. I wanted to make this fun and entertaining, so, I encourage you to listen to the songs mentioned to get a better feel for my story. You may also see some recommended movies and drinks for happy hour.

<u>And just like that this book was born (it's a girl)</u>

One August night I was home blogging with my 14-year-old daughter and I thought to myself: "I have all these entries, love letters, blunders and thoughts about everyday life. Why not put them out there for everyone to read? Who knows, it may bring comfort to someone feeling lonely, warmth to someone feeling cold and laughs to someone feeling sad."
It can also bring happy fingers to someone feeling tipsy, but we won't go there*

The Boy"friends"

The Fulfiller (Introvert) Virgo

He is someone very close to my heart. I have much love for him. He is part of my family and always will be.

His advice to me on life:

"Find your but, don't end your sentences on a bad note."

Ex. So you fell and scraped your knees, BUT at least you have knees.

The Thinker (Introvert) Scorpio
This is my eternal business partner. He is smart and good-looking. We met through a mutual friend. He once told me, "You are my muse" and I was flattered. We bump heads a lot, we talk about Rush Limbaugh and politics and we have totally different views on relationships, love and sex.

His advice to me on life:
"Love is illogical, don't rationalize your emotional stress to justify love."

The Executive (extrovert) Libra
My favorite Libra ever, I confessed to him
once that I had a crush on his brain and he
laughed and told me he had a crush on mine,
too. My confidant, loyal friend, mentor, muse,
he just is. Oh, and he also taught me the word
"Clusterfuck".

His advice to me on life:
"Not my line but it's what I believe. Ready…
Don't sweat the small stuff; everything is
small stuff." –

The Visionary (extrovert) Leo
This is my closest boy friend and everything
I'd love in a man. He is a sexy, confident
Brazilian. We met when I was 27. We've
been there for each other in the good times
and the bad. Together, we were what he
proudly referred to as fun and free*

His advice to me on life:
"Relationships should start out fun and free
and couples should end up complimenting one
another."

The Protector (Introvert) Gemini

This boy I met in high school. I always had a crush on him. He disappointed me when I was 15. I'm 34 now, and, after giving him the chance to redeem himself disappointment has reached a whole new level.

His advice to me on life:
"Life is complex sometimes. Be loyal to your loved ones and put your balls to the wall—don't half-ass it."

The Boy"friend" Diaries

Almost interactions

Just press play: [10,000 Maniacs: Circle Dream]

Relationships are like clay. At first we are lumps, firm and fixed in our outlines. Eventually we change. We reshape our edges and become something new; a tab where there used to be a hole. We straighten out where we were once curved and everything changes. We are shape shifters to a degree.

I'm over us; perhaps that is why I have become another person. You have also become someone else and I realize this is really the only way we began to fall out of love. The fights and tantrums are never really enough to make you fall out of love. Falling out of love requires a shift in perspective, and, thus, a shift in desire. I've grown and changed and all that is left is the nostalgia of what we once were. It's been building. There are days when I wish I could still be the person I once was, the person you once fell in love with. There is no "us" anymore. All that is left is the lingering. In some relationships, it doesn't happen for a long time. We stumble, make mistakes, hurt and grow. We are blown away by crazy/beautiful love affairs and shape shifting interactions. We are becoming and that is enough. Isn't it?

<u>Distance and time</u>
Just press play: [Dashboard Confessionals: Vindicated]

It's difficult to take it all in, I know. We may not have that happy ending because true love never ends but letting go is saying I love you.

I love you enough to watch you walk away, because deep down inside I know that is what you want. We are all afraid of our own reality and our feelings most of all. We talk about how great love is but it isn't always great. Love hurts and feelings are sometimes disturbing. For so long we are taught that pain is evil. But how can we even deal with love if we are afraid to feel pain. Half of love is pain. The pain is what wakes us up. Why do we try to hide our pain when in reality its very presence is proof that we will be stronger? It all depends on how we carry it. That is what really matters. Pain is feeling. Feelings are a part of who we are. If we hide them we are then letting society destroy our reality.
 I'm stronger than my pain.

Unbecoming

I'm not going to take it personally—though it is easier said than done. I have to remember that I can't control how others act, react or deal with issues. I can only control how I react or respond to how I am being treated. Distance and deep breathes because I have to stay true to myself above everything. Walking away-

Past or present, what shall it be?

Just press play [Righteous Brothers: Unchained Melody]

Dear love,

We're all fighting our own demons. Sometimes I feel like I am chained up in an alley like a stray dog that someone has lost or left behind. Those memories of yesterday continue to drive my life into the ground. Unknowingly, I stay chained up in that ally because I don't take the time to grasp that chain in my hands and pull in each link one by one while I stand sturdy on my own two feet. Instead, I hold myself down and drown myself in those memories. I know you don't understand me, and, deep down inside sometimes I think it is easier for you to walk away and not even try to understand. It is easier to carry on your path without me. It is easier to admit to your insides that you love me, but that I am not the one.

It's a bad feeling, however, for me to know that after all the things you've said there is still a chance that you will change your mind about us.

I look at my face in the mirror sometimes and I can see the days that I'm carrying my past pain into the here and now. I look tired and empty. I feel unloved and uncared for. There is no sparkle in my eyes. Things just don't matter, because I don't matter to myself.

Then there are days when I look in the mirror and I'm unbreakable, and, vibrant. On those days, I know that I'm living in the here and now. On those days, I know that I'm not letting my mind carry the past forward into today. On those days I'm free.
But there isn't consistency in my emotions and it isn't because I don't love you or I'm not sure.

It is because we aren't consistently living in the here and now. Because on the days that we are living in the here and now, on those days, I know that I'm not letting my mind carry the past forward into today. On those days I'm free of the inhibitions of yesterday.

I don't want the inhibitions of our minds to chain me up and leave me in that dark alley. I want to walk gracefully hand and hand with you into the beauty of every moment.

I didn't pray for love to find me. I didn't believe in love or soul mates. I didn't believe in any of that and I don't want to be dependent on someone else to help carry me safely into a life of happily ever after.

So what is today going to be for both of us?

Will we walk from our own allies and chains and realize that we're free or will we let our minds carry the past into this day?

One day at a time, one moment at a time that is all we have. Can we make the best of it? Perhaps, if we take the time to embrace what is, I'll thank my lucky stars for this love, I'll understand you are my soul mate and we will live happily ever after, because, right now, I'm standing in that alley alone with that chain in my hand and I can see your silhouette from far away standing there looking back at me. You want to rescue me, you want to free me, and, that's great. But, other times what I see is your shadow walking away from me and leaving me in that dark place, scared, alone, tormented, unloved, unwanted chained up and in love with you. I feel like it is so much easier for you to walk than it is to stay. Because I know it was so much easier for me to be grounded and enclosed in my walls where no one could hurt me, where love wasn't real. In the end, however, I allowed myself to be vulnerable again and I let you into my world. I love you, as much as you love me-

So, what's it going to be?
Hold,
Me.

The truth shall settle.
Just press play: [Peter Gabriel: *In Your Eyes*]

Dear love,

Our truth is our individual gift to the world around us. Who are we to deny someone the growth that may be incurred from the truth?

Do we really like disrespecting ourselves by not speaking up and speaking out what we know to be true?

Truth requires speaking out from that vulnerable place inside that feels something, then usually edits down into silence and transforms into rage. The truth takes balls. So here are mine:

I'm afraid of losing you and I really need you to know that.
I've fallen in love with you.
You give me butterflies.
I feel scared and unworthy of what the future has in store for us.
I like to watch you smoke from the sliding door in the back yard. I enjoy the silence of your silhouette.
I'm afraid that if you know truthfully that I'm not as tough as I look on the outside you'll leave me.
You take my breath away.
I feel disconnected from you at times.
I love the way your skin feels bare and close to me.

I feel like you talk at me, and not really to me depending on how you feel about the topic of conversation.

I daydream about the day you ask me to marry you.

I don't want the story of your past to become the story of our present.

Every time I see a rose I smile once for you and once for the beauty in it and in you.

It bothers me that you let other people become you and you allow them to separate you from those that you love.

When I look into your eyes, you're insides and mine are in deep conversation.

I don't think you really believe that we are going to make it.

I constantly ask myself how I fell so deeply, so madly and so unexpectedly.

I really do have separation anxiety.

When we say goodbye it always feels like it's going to be the last time I'm ever going to see you.

I fear that you have the ability to do what is least expected so I'm kept on my toes and I carefully watch my step.

I tread carefully because I'm afraid that you are able to easily carry on without me.

I'm scared to buy you things because I'm afraid you'll give them back to me one day when you leave me.

I worry that you'll forget me.

I ask myself what will be of me if I become part of your story, part of your past.

When I think about us, I see a series of old Polaroid pictures with captions.

I have nightmares that I'm walking barefoot on a beach full of eggshells instead of sand and in this dream you're on a sailboat and you don't see me or the eggshells.

I think about the things you've said to me when you've been upset. I know you didn't mean them, but the words are heavy and they haven't fully lifted from my insides.

I still think of her.

Sometimes I feel like the more honest I am with you, the less you believe in us and the easier it is for you to walk away.

I'm afraid of losing you and I really need you to know my truths.

Wondering,
Me.

<u>Will it ever end?</u>
Just press play: [Limp Bizkit: My Way]

How much longer? How many more sleepless nights of meaningless bullshit? How many more times am I going to have to endure the lingering, wondering, wishing, hoping, waiting, longing, missing, wanting, needing ... how much more? What is it going to take for you to step it up? What are you waiting for? I think that you are way too caught up in crap to even care what is going on inside me. I'm so disillusioned.

Quality reality TV = my life
Just press play: [DJ Nancy Starr: Ego Trip 42 Podcast on iTunes]

Like my friend Hayli would say: Never Ever A Dull Moment. The "ever" puts it in a league of its own.

Daydreaming and dumbfounded
Just press play: [The Killers: Leave The Bourbon On The Shelf]

Dear love,

I missed you today when I awoke from my slumber only to find my heart empty and my eyes still tired. My dreams are slowly becoming as I sleepwalk steadfast through out my day wondering how you are and why I am not the one. And they are most definitely bittersweet, like the rest of me. I'm a little scared. I know I shouldn't say that. Although I will admit it is a thought that frequently visits the back of my mind lately. I shouldn't feel this way, I know and that isn't even the hardest part; the hardest part is that I did this knowingly. You have somehow changed me and I am not sure what that means exactly. I certainly do not know you long enough to feel this way but I certainly do long to know you better, perhaps, because I enjoy you deeply. I'm not good at relationships. You make me feel uncertain, awkward, weird, vulnerable and a few other things that I'm too prude to write. There are so many reasons I shouldn't tell you this: I have left the broken wreckage of relationships behind me. I couldn't stand to ever hurt you and though I am very concerned that you will hurt me I have taken the chance and fallen anyway. I hope that you can forgive me.

Your Muse,
(I'm flattered) –

<u>I like you as long as you just like me...</u>

The Human Mind is Fascinating...Understanding how we make decisions, how we form preferences, how we think about the future is not only intellectually interesting, it can also help us understand the dynamics of conversation... "People perceive reciprocity in two different flavors- when it comes to romance. In a romantic context we like only those who like us back exclusively or at least we try." – The Science of Speed Dating.

<u>Wordplay</u>

For someone that really impressed me with intelligence, you've really disappointed me with your banter.
<u> And the academy award goes to…</u>
Just press play: [Lykke Li: Little Bit]

Dear love,

I'm only scared because I believe that I am limited and I am only feeling lonely because I have stopped doing things. I'm bored because I've stopped following my heart and overwhelmed because I believed all the meaningless illusions you created to lure me in.

Reality Check,
Me.

<u>The Pussy Chase-</u>
Just press play: [Mickey Avalon: My Dick]

I was confused about men and their (un) complicated thinking process. So in my search for clarification I learned some valuable lessons about boys, thanks to, you.

1. It is incredibly difficult to get noticed in the constant barrage of media and everyday traffic; thus it is essential to stand out, be singled out and get noticed!
2.Finding the love of your life or your girlfriend is more about your pursuits than chasing her.

3. Use props, your car and shoes matter.

4. Monet and Broadway get you laid.

5. We pursue that which retreats from us.

6. Money is important.

So this is how men should really think according to you. You are brilliant. Thank you.

Observing...
Just Press Play: [The Soup Dragons: I'm Free]

Jellyfish.
Maybe we humans need to learn from them: Live in the present and just float gracefully in this sea of life. Enjoy the ride. Don't fight against the current.
I like to believe that jellyfish do have a soul ... and that their soul can be seen on the outside ... pure, and, transparent. No lies, no attachments, no pain. Just living a pure, authentic, genuine, natural, clear life.

Jamming to life,
Me

Vie
Just press play: [Coldplay: The Scientist]

You and me and never us: A series of almost interactions.

The radio played a sweet song today and I smiled because I thought of you. It was an old song that I can't remember now. I don't quite understand why I can't remember the name of the song but I can't seem to forget other things.

Interesting how the mind tries not to remember while the heart never forgets. Stay in my heart forever. Because though I tell my mind to forget you the truth is that I don't want my heart to forget you and me and I tell it that there is still hope ... although I know there isn't. Perhaps I am only fooling my insides but when I don't know what to turn to the pain of your void is all that I have. I find you have penetrated my sub-conscious mind my thoughts either stem from you or branch from you. It may sound crazy but it is true. Quantum Entanglement and the Philosophy within Wonderland is what is keeping me as sane as I can possibly be, and, of course, staying drunk on my writing so that reality cannot destroy me.

It matters not...

"I am the master of my fate: I am the captain of my soul." - Invictus
Feels good to be able to own those.
Life: Nothing but love for you.

In all the wrong ways

The fragile keep secrets gathered in pockets and they will free them for nothing, not a watch or cheap locket. They're scared of forever, they hide and then seek, they do not seem weak and their silence speaks. My memories are hostage within my thoughts. I'm holding on to forget me not. Do I ring a bell? I'm hoping you'll tell. Are we on our way? Will we be okay? I'm out of bed; you're in my head. You make the choices, not those strange voices. Don't leave me here with my secrets. I may have acted in illogical lapses and I know I'm not talking, but can't you hear me?

Ahoy mates and soul mates

There is a unique ability and a fearless nature in the souls ability to explore the infinite depths of its own abyss. It is what allows you to be free and clear of judgment and perception prejudices. This is a trait that very few have. To be compelled, to extrapolate and eviscerate from the clutches of those around you that are only interested in changing what you are.

<u>Take your time.</u>

Now that I have reconciled, I understand that all this time I was the one misunderstanding you.

Movie must: [Pretty Woman]

<u>In the tangles again</u>
Just press play: [Aqua Lung: Brighter Than Sunshine]

Dear love,

You have stolen my August. You hid disguised of innocent humor and pushed me back to that place where last we dreamed in make pretend. You draped an irresistible velvety lather before my eyes and then tripped me. I fell, you know? I went for it, reopening my wounds with my predictable pain and now

I'm left keeping the salty sea away from the scratches.
You have risen from the depths of my heart and whispered your way into the light in some futile attempt to whisk me along again. You sat there singing our bittersweet song and luring me with your musky scent and brilliant blunders.
You act like we haven't been through this. You've torn me open again. But don't worry. I'll fight harder this time to continue loving you.

The finer things
Just press play: [Kate Nash: I Hate Seagulls]

Dear love,

You are:
The smell of coffee brewing in the early morning.
The tea cup at the edge of my paper napkin.
The click sound of all my cameras.
The green light during rush hour traffic.
The last piece of sharp cheddar.
The sun shining and the free-flowing crisp air.
The snooze button on the alarm clock of my life.

The night sky in my favorite city.
The site of happy people.
The last glass of Chianti waiting for me in my
slumber.
The sweet songs playing on the radio.
The scent of patchouli, my favorite.
The blanket fresh out the dryer.
The unbalanced rush in my irregular heart
beat.
The one I love.
Fade into me.

Vent
Just press play [John Mayer: Say]

Dear love,

At the end of the day it's better to say too
much than to never say what you need to say.
 Happy and full
Just press play: [Mazzy Starr: Fade Into You]

I think you are brilliant and wonderful, much
more than half the people that I've ever met.
You are smart, funny, interesting,
complicated, moral, real and courteous.
Sleep, Dream, Reality, Repeat.

<u>Finite or infinite?</u>

What is a condition that is not limited to a specific set of values but can vary infinitely within a continuum? I love these questions. But what I love more is that you always know the answer. You're such a nerd.

<u>All roads lead to love.</u>
Just press play: [Sting: Shape Of My Heart]

She fell in love with a brilliant man once; a man with a deep theory on emotions and the thinking process.

Brilliant Man:
"Errant thoughts provoke haphazard decisions fueled by emotions and not necessarily thought. Errant thoughts are really emotions that should be ignored all together and not acted upon haphazardly."

Inexperienced and dumbfounded, she loved him. She thought errantly, and made haphazard decisions fueled by love struck emotions that rarely underwent any real thought process and only being loved this passionately did he carefully realize that there was no other way to love or be loved in return.

<u>Lost in London.</u>
Just press play: [Lykke Li: Time Flies]

The days have passed so quickly. I'm not sure I understand how this can be so different from my reality. I feel like time has temporarily paused and if I look back I can see everything through a transparent glass sphere enclosing a miniaturized scene of us with a pretty landscape. My feelings activate this scene. Sets of pins revolve around my heart, they prick the steel fence that surrounds it and the result is that of a magical noise. A built-in music box, of sorts, and the song that plays is bittersweet. How can this be real? I'm in disbelief and so unaware.

<u>Marc, where art thou?</u>

I am looking out for Marc, a fictional character of a dwindling breed that I have created in my mind. He is perfect.
You were prefect to me, too. You were so good at pretending.
What the fuck were you thinking? What the fuck am I thinking? Marc!

Shot time: [Rumplemintz]

<u>More than one side</u>
Just press play: [Neon Trees: Animal]

Dear love,

There is a different perspective to every story that is told. Just because you have trouble seeing another's point doesn't mean that you should make "absolute" statements. There are no "absolute" perspectives.

Chances are people aren't going to see things your way and because we are free to have our own perspective we should always mean what we say.
Shifting Perspectives.
 <u>Plebian</u>
Just press play: [Lykke Li: Possibility]

We are all like wild flowers; shocked and hurt by actions but in the end you still gave me more than you took away. How quickly the middle became the end.

<u>Perpetually</u>

Forever is a long time, but I wouldn't mind spending it by your side

The difference between disaster and deliverance is life.
Just press play: [Postal Service: Such Great Heights]

Life is a condition that distinguishes organisms. Life is manifested by growth through metabolism and reproduction. We communicate, and we have the ability to adapt to any environment through changes that originate internally. We are liberated. We are alive.

They say that Life on Earth was made possible by the death of stars. Atoms, like carbon and oxygen, were expelled in the last few dying gasps of stars after their final supplies of hydrogen fuel were used up. How this star-stuff came together to form life is still a mystery. We are all star- stuff" - Carl Sagan

We are all made of mystifying elements. We are multi-cellular organisms, creating on the polychromatic canvas of life.

This is the "Art" of life. Some of us are beautiful paintings, perfectly colored and magically unique. Some of us are lifeless and unfinished and some are in between. We are the creators of our painting. We make the choices to accent our canvas. We decide what we experience to enlighten not only what we see, but what others see as well.

Everyday, our painting is different. Some days everything that we manifest is perfect; on other days, it seems like we may no longer have that pretty color that we found just yesterday, and so we are forced to make the best of this "Art" with what we have, we are forced to make the best of our ingenious magnum opus.

We are not allowed to ask why, but we are expected to proceed with caution so that we create not just any meaningless dabble but one that defines our very life, our minuscule meaningful masterpiece.

Life as we know it today, the creation of evolution, unfolding, changing, progressing. Sometimes life is and sometimes it just isn't.

And for these reasons

We are who we are for a lot of reasons. Perhaps we'll never know why. But even though we don't have the power to choose where we came from we can still choose where we go. We can still do things and we can still try to feel okay about them.

At this point the only thing that still makes it a part of my life is that I keep thinking about it.

Pyrrhic-victory
Just press play: [Third Eye Blind: How's It Gonna' Be]

And in the end the pictures remain—and what I've lost is proof of what I've gained.

<u>Post Pangea – My rendition of a 15th century love letter</u>
Just press play: [Debussy: Clair De Lune]

Dear love,

Sooner or later I will have to find something else to take my mind off of you. Whatever it is, I hope it hurts just as much. This, my very last love letter to you, hurts enough for now. Here I sit drinking water, preparing for 90 minutes in a heated room where I will punish my body to the point of exhaustion and feel pain like never before. The pain stills that bird in my ribcage and allows me time to be inside my own mind alone. It is the only time I have where I can resist thinking of you.

Whatever else can be said for us in the long road of this love, I will say that I've never stopped loving you. I will die loving you as fiercely as I ever have, as passionately as I ever have, where tendrils of pain creep up my spine and into my ribcage, choking the very breathe from my body. That love has been enough to carry me this far and it will have to do for me if my future is without you.

That is how I feel you, still. I will have to adapt to the empty feeling of "without you"- I wish for the gentle rise and fall of my chest as I try to have you with me, sobbing with relief, that which I will never know. Instead I just lose myself in the void my heart has without its counter part.

I keep telling myself that this is going to subside though I am well aware it will not. Tomorrow will come and I will have to adjust. I will have to force myself to walk and I know it won't be easy. I hope reading this is hard for you. Half of love is pain. I try to inhale profoundly, but my breath is interrupted. I can feel my insides speak softly to my soul. I allow that voice to take over me. The sound of your voice is faint now. This is so hard on me. I have to hold on because I know it will hurt more and longer before it ever goes away. Still, I am afraid of becoming numb to this pain and learning to live without you.

The thin streams of dull sunlight filtering through my cracked blinds have discovered my bed again cold and wanting. I press my eyelids and I think "God If you can hear me, take my life, take my limbs, take my sanity, take anything but please, don't take my love."

My bed remains discontent even with my soothing promise of a peaceful sleep tonight. My weight sinks into the cold, buckling softness and huddles trembling beneath stiff sheets. My feelings take their time to make me miserable, prodding constantly at my insides, twisting me even as I attempt futilely to drift into sleep, stirring me even in my slumber, and lacing my pillow with visions that strain and buckle my overworked dream catcher. Thoughts peel my words from my body. Their pages ripping and in their pieces I lay incomplete, jagged and bare.

I remain at a loss of what to do to calm my savage mind. My feelings have their own entity and they threaten me and stand poised to do me more harm, warranting that their demands are not met. You have made it quite clear that you have no interest in them, for they have neither the weight nor the parts to make you surrender. So please, I beg you, hurry back; soothe this wound for it hurts and it longs to be sutured with your love again. I have yet to sleep since you have gone. My feelings are anxious and vehement. Bring your body to warm them, your weight to soften them, your arms to defend them and me from their next assault. I fear what evil they have in store for me while you are gone.

Is this too much for you? I'm sorry for my shrewish tone. It was an unpleasant discovery that I stumbled upon when I lost you. Have I lost you yet? I don't want my wounds to fester. I'm afraid they will, and I thought you should know the ice you left in my heart has made me frigid and numb, but the wound remains open and hurtful. My thoughts plan the demise of our love and I will suffer a great deal more if my wound heals from lack of being able to love you. So in return I offer you my words. They, and I, are yours. This is my very last love letter to you. It hurts enough for now.

Time
Just press play: [Paolo Nutini: Last Request]

Dear love,

One thousand four hundred and sixty days later, I still wonder why time is the best storyteller of all time.

<u>Wild card</u>
Just press play: [Antonio Carlos Jobim: Girl From Ipanema]

Dear love,

I love surprise endings.

<u>Diaphanously, imprisoned</u>
Just Press Play: [Kaoma: Lambada]

Dear love,

I feel wounded, and I am left to question my own motives for this self-inflicted pain. I don't want to love you anymore; not if you aren't going to love me the way that I want to be loved. It is conditional I realize that, but I can't do it. I'm hurting, and I can't ever explain the kind of pain I feel because it hurts so much that mere words are not capable of ever doing it any justice. Most of the day I'm unbalanced from trying so hard to ignore the voice in my head. I've asked myself why at least one thousand times. My insides are devoid; I've told you that before. I'm broken, and I know that I cannot ever be fixed and it

isn't because I'm not able. It is because I realize that it isn't ever going to go away. I enable this craziness, despite the circumstances and there are times that I actually feel worse, because I'm the one that has made the choice not to talk to you.
It is selfish, I know, but if I am forced to move forward and steadfast, I fear that I will not be able to do that if you are left to linger, I'm sorry. Maybe if we were normal there would be a chance, but we are far from normal and I am done taking chances. I am the one left watching you walk away every time. I am the one still standing every time you look back and contemplate whether or not you've made the right decision; and when you return, and, you always do, it is validated. I am there through the wind. I am there through the rain. I am there always.

So, yes, the answer is yes. I am inconsolable. I know you pretend not to understand that. I've noticed the pattern in your behavior; how quickly you are to respond when something I feel bothers you, because you well know that your actions are the cause. You pretend that it's not possible for someone to have the power to make you feel a certain way. So, you belittle those feelings instead of putting yourself through the distress that you in fact are their cause. You make it a point to remind me how amazing I am, but you forget to remind me that I'm not amazing enough for you. The thing is, I didn't forget either of those things. Don't try to make me feel better. Inconsolable, remember? That means there is no need for you to try.

Sometimes when I'm driving in traffic, I look out the window and I tell myself "I'm doing well and managing adequately." But instantaneously I hear the distant laughter of that voice in my mind. I try to dispel the nauseating reality that I am living and I say to myself epigrammatically: How quickly things have changed. I wish that I could fix myself to what you find is perfect for you. If you would only bite your tongue and let me love you. Just then the voice whispers "Why?"

And when traffic is suddenly at a stand still I lower my window and I stick my hand out with my palm facing upward and as my hand divides the cold dry wind that hits it, I close my eyes for just a second and I imagine my beating heart on the palm of my very hand amidst all the chaos that surrounds it and I can see it clearly, and it feels just like my hand does. I want to pull it inside and make it warm again. The thing is that it's already inside where the cold dry airs permanently resides—wish I could just take it out. But since I can't I have no choice but to allow it to beat, to pump the blood that rushes through my veins feeding my desires, weakening my resistance, sustaining my unfulfilled aspirations, allowing me to stumble unstably—and I haven't a say. I cannot force my mind to fulfill its request to resist from loving you.

I think of you throughout the day. Come to think of it there are always sporadic moments when your physique appears in my thoughts and they scatter everywhere; everywhere but where they are suppose to be; and just before I can confine them back to my painful and unpleasant reality I pause and tell myself "I wish it was bittersweet, like it used to be" and I remember the old us—we have never been fun and free like you've wanted us to be, but we have always "been", always, except now.

"I'm here, I'm not going anywhere". I should know by now that we are a false pretense that I have created by hanging on to your words; words like those. I'm losing myself. I toss and turn at night and I wonder if you think of me. I wonder if you think of what this is doing to my insides. How can we balance if we are always at this oddly pointed knife? It is inevitable we are bound to fall off. It isn't real. We aren't real. It is some fictional love story that I have created for sake of the hopeless romantic that lives imprisoned within my soul with orders to love just you. It's sick and fictitious and that I am aware of you are not Shakespeare and this is not some rendition of 15th century love story where we spin viciously until we are at some point rescued and rewarded with a life of "happily ever after."

I'm sleep waking through life, it's lucid, nonetheless, and catatonic and echoless, too— I have to wake at some point and look up to see the edge of the knife we were standing on. The worse part is standing up, and dusting myself off, only to be reprimanded by that distant voice that whispers so unkindly "Come on, you've know this all along, I told you so" and I have to swallow my pride without being prejudice and wallow in the conviction of my indecision. I hate it.

As I sit and I write the tangible truth is slowly resurfacing. Resurfacing: I don't like that word. When things resurface it means that they where once peripheral and somehow they were submerged and lost for sometime, even if for a moment something has to be lost to all of a sudden resurface. When things are on the edge they always run the risk of being unstable, falling off or being lost. Yes, they can resurface but why can't they just remain on the outer boundaries of the circle consistently; instead of balancing on the extremities, leaving room for the uninviting surrender and for the plummet of the breakdown? It would be so uncomplicated. If it were all up to me; we would always be evidently, secure on the apparent exterior surface, never having to resurface, meaning always and consistently present. After all, isn't that how we are supposed to live, always consistently present?

We are temporary and at this point my vision has become blurry. I'm not sure what the end result of this will be, if it will even be at all. Nature sure played a deceitful trick on me if this is it, after I religiously followed the course not minding the forecast, weathering the storm, carrying my backpack, feeling unwavering while staring at my vision clearly despite the unfamiliar and unfriendly surrounding and against all odds.

As irrational as it seems this is deeply liberating. The very act frees me from the tyranny of my internal critic, from the uneasiness that likes to dress itself up and parade around like a circus of rational hesitation. You remove my inner critic, the barrier to my life and inside all the mystification I become able to watch you walk away time and time again—fearless, undoubted, worry free without regrets, focused, ready and without me and it hurts so madly to watch the beginning of our end.

Perhaps
Just press play: [Boz Scaggs: Look What You've Done]

Dear love,

Perhaps my uncanny ability to hear the smallest stir of you is what drives me running into your arms. I lay and wait most mornings, half asleep half awake, taking pleasure in the stillness, wanting to stretch out and touch you with my toes, to feel your warmth with me. I wonder if you know your own propensity. I am wanting and waiting—I close my eyes and this feeling creates a soft song in my soul. I see you facing my side, your right arm outstretched beneath my pillow. I have never felt safer than when I'm lying in that warm space you've made just for me against your chest, the soft rushing of your breath against my ear.

For me, the quiet comprehension of lying next to you, and, the gentle affection expressed in your touch, carries more love than my heart has ever known. I feel like a daffodil, caught under your penumbra of gladness, drowned in your humble brilliance. "Love's a fool's dance," and thus I shall be dancing forever because of you. This love has again crept upon me, with its velvety paws. I don't know why it is that I fall in love with you, but I do. I just see you and hear you and even the trifling irritations make me fall.

You came to me in a dream last night, again. It seems like every time we fall apart, my heart finds a way to bring you back to me, somehow. I was alone and lost somewhere strange and unknown. I felt broken and scared and the musical sounds of your voice lead me through the path of least resistance, to find you there solid, confident and waiting for me. A weight was lifted from within when I looked up and saw your perfectly chiseled face. Your expression was quite different this time. It was serene and spiritually sound, as where you. Your broad shoulders amaze me still, and the way you look at me when excitement seeps your veins creates an eminent passion deep within me and all I can think to myself is "I never want this feeling to go away".

Some time has passed in this dream, since last we spoke or saw each other. Some time has passed since I felt close to you, and close to us. Why is it that we fall apart each time we do and why do you leave in this horribly messy way. I feel you in the rain, I hear you in my words and I smell you in my sheets. How do you do this thing you do so well to me? How do you find your way into my soul and see that when you do, you had been there all along? Your touch has once again erased your lies from my wounded life and though I prayed for your return, I have become lucid and my insides are tired and sore.

The dark mists of the past leaves our separate souls standing together in a chill, clinging gray fog and in this grey fog our insides are blurry and unclear, just like our future and past. The walls of my imagination are playing tricks on me again and I'm not sure that I will make it out this time whole. The deep fierce aching and rising fear and the cries of needing you have dissolved into the air. Something slips from within without choice or question, and wraps itself around me forever, like the breath of the moon.

My heart desires to see you again. My feelings for you are unbounded by any rules and laws and they have been for quite some time. I find myself in the deepest of thoughts these days. I've been praying to God to please arrange the circumstances in such a way that this would be easier this time around.

I realize that by even asking for such a thing is selfish and wrong in many ways. The uncertainty has me lost, confused and apologizing for my thoughtless actions or inactions. You've seduced my heart again and captured it and the window has closed now. I know what I did wrong. I love you, I always have and my heart is completely yours.

Movie must: [About Last Night]

The secret weapon
Just press play: [Jay-Z: Brush Your Shoulders Off]

Dear love,

I realize that in order to love you fully I must embrace the "Band-Aids" and I'm not sure I can do that. So, in honor of the stage 5 clingers that linger, I'll walk away, and I've given our window of opportunity an expiration date—38 on the 28th. Get ALL the wiggles out. Until then-

Complimenting us,
Me.

Lead me, love me
Just press play: [Foreigner: I Want To Know What Love Is]

Dear love,

I don't know what I'm getting into; here is what I do know:
I'm letting you lead me. I'm letting you love me. Love me and lead me blindly into this place. I'm so afraid, not because I don't want to go, but because I can't stop myself from going.

I'm struggling with my insides, perhaps because you've unraveled them so perfectly and they are so safe while they are loving you, deeply. I've tucked my heart away in our last kiss; please don't misplace it for I fear I won't be able to breathe if I can't continue loving you and wanting this. I'm taken by every moment. I watch our past memories replay in my mind, and, although they are blurry they are still colorful.

I've created a mental flipbook of this love story and the pictures vary gradually from one page to the next. It must be because I enjoy lingering in every moment so much that I want to dance in those very moments with you as along as possible. Sometimes I turn the imaginary rapidly to the beat of my racing heart and what I feel brings the images to life.

I watch us in this imaginary flipbook, we are evolving so beautifully and our emotions are fueling the change in these pictures. They are so perfectly illustrated in this hopeless romantic's mind of mine.

I promise to keep you intoxicated in this passion, so long as you promise to love me and lead me carefully out of suspended animation and into a reality of happily ever after... no pressure. Do I love you, you ask? Yes, master.

<u>Make a mess of my insides; I want to feel disoriented in this lust.</u>
Just press play: [The Temper Trap: Sweet Disposition]

Dear love,

I'm not the perfect fit nor am I looking for the perfect fit. I want a mirror. Show me everything that is holding me back. Bring me to my own attention so I can make the changes I need to make in my life. Be the most important person that I have ever met. Tear down my walls and help me awaken from my dream state. I don't want forever. I want for right now, for this moment. I want the rush of being. I want to bathe in the nothingness of this moment. I want you to make a mess of my insides. I want to feel disoriented in this lust.

You've come into my life to reveal another layer of myself to me. So shake me up, show me my obstacles and my addictions, carve your way into my heart and show me a higher state of consciousness.

<u>Fight for your right</u>
Just press play: [The Cure: Lullaby]

Welcome to the era of unprecedented bullshit. Actually, it's not so much the end product but the process by which it is created. The basis of how situations become circumstances. It sounds complicated but in reality it is just bullshit. At the end of the day, life goes on and nothing can stop the evolution of our destiny—nothing, no matter what it is. I wont ever be the one to cry wolf.

<u>WTF</u>

[Open Scene]:

Because my life is like a TV show, I feel like when it is all over and everything is going perfectly I will get the infamous shoulder tap and then I'll hear this deep TV/Radio personality voice tell me, "Star Roman, you're on the Roman show." And, right then and there, I come to the realization that all the suffering, all the obstacles, all the setbacks, all that I've worked so hard to accomplish will somehow be worthless and pure entertainment for others.

Long sigh of relief. (Brought to you by Wonder Woman)

[End Scene]:

Movie must: [The Truman Show]

Free your words

We feel them before we say them. Careful. It can get a little scary.

Game over

The only reason we hold back is because we think we have an endless amount of chances or that there will always be one more. As time disappears into the past and life goes on, those chances will run out and you'll either live with eternal happiness for being brave, or eternal regret for holding back. So take chances, make mistakes. That's how you grow. Pain nourishes your courage. You have to fail in order to practice being brave. So, what if you are beyond being accepted by the norm? What is normal anyway? Be original. Originality implies that you are bold enough to go beyond what is accepted.

Shot time: [Sex With An Alligator]

<u>It's a bird, it's a plane, it's…</u>
Just press play: [Ludacris: Move Bitch]

Motivation: The force that initiates, guides and maintains goal-oriented behaviors. Motivation is what causes us to act. It is what causes us to take action, whether to grab a snack to reduce hunger or enroll in college to earn a degree. The forces that lie beneath motivation can be biological, social, emotional or cognitive in nature. It involves the biological, emotional, social and cognitive forces that activate behavior. Why do you do things?

Motivation. And, what keeps you doing them? RESULTS. Dalé.

Blah, blah, blah- or words?
Just press play: [Deelight: Groove Is In The Heart]

You should own the words you say, because those words come with a responsibility. When you say hurtful words, those that are blurted out without thinking, they also come with a responsibility, one that you carry like a weight. You simply cannot un-say those. I am far from perfect but I always own my words because I know at some point I may have to eat them.

Terribly In Love

Have you ever been in love? It makes you vulnerable, rips open your chest and makes your heart beat erratically. This means that someone can get in and make a mess of your insides.

Still, so messy on the inside,
Me.

Shot time: [Bellini]

<u>What dreams may come</u>
Just press play: [This will destroy you: The
World is Our _____]

I washed up on a waterfront filled with the old
shipwrecks along the seashore that slowly
began disappearing one by one into the salty
sea and on to a harbor with a dark city
alongside it. I, too, noticed that the ships were
not moving on their own volition; they were
being tugged by a beautiful mermaid instead.
A crowd began to gather at this phenomenon.
The harbor was misty and the city was unclear
and deserted. A strong wind started
transcending.

Seeing these ships made me worry, though
I'm not sure why. Perhaps it was the black
muck that began to stir as the mermaid
struggled to make it safely on to the harbor.

The resources at play seemed scant and the situation almost impossible, one after the other the wrecks were being pulled to sea and an amazing light bathed the town each time one made it successfully to the harbor.

My amazement grew when I found myself at sea and near some ropes in attempt to pull the very last ship. It was a pirate ship, dark and mysterious. The anchors were tied to its sides and they suddenly came to life with feeling and personality.

I noticed them and they immediately noticed me. It was a strange encounter. I knew that should they jump the ship would then be anchored and moving it near the harbor would be more impossible than it already seemed, for I was dumbfounded to find that the ropes tied to the anchors were no bigger than shoe laces and that at one point a dried broken branch from a nearby tree served as a pin to secure them.

Why was I the conductor of this symphony? I started to tire, and feel weak and before I knew it the anchors took their leap and I realized that all along they were just waiting for my weaknesses to settle to secure the ship far from the harbor and in the fury of the open sea.

Every time I saw each ship reach the harbor the city lights would shine ever so beautifully. The mist started clearing out slowly. I could see the mermaid from afar, wanting to help me with this last ship, but she too was afraid of the anchors. I didn't understand where I stood or how I was able to be so close to this ship and yet so far from the harbor. From where I was standing, I could not see. The waves were so much bigger than I was; it was difficult to look down without losing my balance. I was barely clothed and barefoot. Every time the waves would crash against me, I carefully stood up despite the coldness in my chest and the prickling under my feet.

I kept thinking of ways to reach the harbor. I wanted so badly to tug this ship to a safe place. I wanted to befriend the anchors. I felt I had to. I somehow lifted and to my own disbelief I was aboard the pirate ship now and I felt a gentle voice tell me, "I know they hurt. How did you get these eggshells at the bottom of your feet? They've been there for so long … this salt will help your wounds fester." I was confused and disoriented. I felt sick and afraid.

I was tired and distressed by the time I woke up and this was the only wreck that was left at sea. These emotions I felt in the dream were still with me when I opened my eyes and I found myself safely tangled in bed sheets. Why do we dream? What purpose do dreams serve? We spend so much time dreaming there has to be an explanation. And, if there isn't then why do we dream? Are the images conveying a message? Are the thoughts and emotions a way of our subconscious mind giving us a signal of what's coming? Dreams: They can be extraordinarily vivid or very vague. They can be filled with emotion be it fear or joy, frightening images or beautiful scenery. They can be focused and understandable or unclear and confusing.

But the question remains...
Why do we dream?

Carpe Diem

After a long night of impartial thinking, of the truths and after much calling upon the higher beings to give me the strength to seize the moment of truth, today I find myself at peace, by both principles and reason so I can gracefully embrace what life has in store for me.

Shot time: [Snake Eyes]

<u>Taming the beast</u>
Just press play: [Limp Bizkit: Break Stuff]

When you lose your cool, people lose respect for you. Whether you are right or wrong, all that is remembered is that you acted irrationally, you yelled and screamed and you lost control over your emotions. People may fear your rage, but they do not respect you as a result of it.
Fear and respect are two different things.
Fear: a distressing emotion aroused by impending danger, evil, pain, whether it is real or imagined; the feeling or condition of being afraid.
Respect: esteem for or a sense of the worth or excellence of a person, a personal quality or ability, or something considered as a manifestation of a personal quality or ability.
Just pointing out the difference.
<u>The love we deserve</u>

Just press play: [Gregory And The Hawk: Boats And Birds]

Dear love,

I deserve the right kind of love, the kind of love that makes me happy. The fantastic love that's in books and movies. Even if we aren't together forever, I want to look back and never regret having fallen in love with you.

Closer
I write to give myself the strength I need to accept the things I'm afraid of.

Don't let it get the best of you.
Just press play: [The Shins: Caring Is Creepy]

Dear love,

Often, situations can seem overwhelming. I know you may not know what to do. Talk to me, you know me well, you trust me don't you? Sometimes we have to swallow our pride but most of the time we will feel better. Learn about yourself, your likes and your dislikes. Those are the things that can help you avoid certain circumstances in the future.

Doing the same thing over and over again while expecting a different result is insanity. We learn from our circumstances. It is also how we help others. This is life, we learn as we go along and we are going to be okay. Aren't we?

Sweet, sweet love
Just press play: [Adele: Rolling In The Deep]

Dear love,

How did you do that? How did you twist and turn my thoughts?

Tangerine trees and marmalade skies

Dear love,

Lie. That's what I think about everything you've ever said to me so far. Everyday you make it more evident that you are incapable of being the one simply because you just don't want to put your part. Sure, it requires effort, but if you can't commit to the well being of yourself for you, then how the hell can you be 100% all in for anyone—especially for me? As it is, my expectations of us are already so high (for me). No Pressure, you've walked before. I wouldn't be surprised if you walked again.

Following the yellow brick road,
Me.

Movie must: [Eternal Sunshine Of The Spotless Mind]

<u>WHAT IS IT THAT YOU WANT FROM ME?</u>
Just press play: [Lady Gaga: Speechless]

Dear love,

Tell me what it is that you want? Take a moment to explain to me exactly what you would like for me to do, because, to be quite honest with you; I'm not sure if I know anymore. Don't toy with me and my heart because I promise you this: You will not be able to blink your fucking eyes without thinking about how badly you fucked up.

<u>Are you?</u>

Dear love,

It's easy to take off your clothes and sleep with someone; people do it all the time. But opening your soul to someone, letting them into your spirit, thoughts, fears, future, hopes, dreams, that's the true essence of being naked*

Bare,
Me.

Movie must: [Garden State]

Soul mates

Me: Besties, I spoke to the dry cleaning today. After all, he paid for it. I feel close to him when I'm close to the dry cleaning. Is that a little psycho? Don't tell anyone.
Besties: Can you say "interfriendtion"?
Me: Who's buying?

Movie must: [Sex And The City 1 and 2]

A conversation of mind and heart

Just press play: [Imogen Heap: Hide And Seek]

Heart: He's hilarious.
Mind: He's world's biggest asshole.
Heart: He makes me race.
Mind: He ruins my day.
Heart: He saves you at the last minute.
Mind: He's driving you crazy, he's out of his mind.
Heart: You hate him; he's everything you want.

In between,
Me.

Wise words from my intern:

"I live in Grey motherfucker so move in or pack your black and white bags."- A. Toledo
Giving my "grey" matters a work out,
Me.

Buh-bye

Just press play: [Two Door Cinema Club: Something Good Can Work]

Dear writers block,
 We all know that it is always all so bittersweet for me ... your farewell could not stay far behind. They say that artists have to feel to create. I can tell you that my most amazing creations were born out of pure misery and heartache. So, I, of course, agree. For the last few days, I couldn't write; perhaps, because I didn't feel enough. Now, that I have submerged myself into the rabbit hole of madness, (again) I shall write. It hurts to part ways with you like this. But there will be a great work of art in your honor.

Forever the artist,
Me.

Hialeah Helan vs. NYC Tolle
Just press play: [Frank Sinatra: NY, NY]

Because sometimes being shaken back into reality is the only way we really, truly understand. Hialeah Helan all the way.

Minus "The Pulp" Thank you,

Me.

Insides and outsides
Just press play: [Phoenix: Lisztomania]
What is happening to my insides? Is it that I
feel too much or perhaps I feel the wrong
ways? My insides and outsides aren't
matching up. Do anyone's?
Is our personality the difference between our
insides and outsides?

Not understanding
Just press play: [Amy Winehouse: Back To
Black]

Dear love,

I hate to feel misunderstood. I do not like not
being able to communicate. It doesn't make
me feel like we are making progress.
Problems don't just go away. Haven't you
noticed? They just go into a temporary sleep
state, where they later become creepy
zombies that haunt you forever. I don't want
to be haunted by misunderstandings that were
never brought to the table and made crystal
clear and apparent. Actually, I don't want to
be haunted by anything. I'm tired of being

haunted by things that I have left unsaid. They have come back to haunt me in my sleep, in my thoughts, in my creativity, in my relationships, in my friendships and in my life long goals and aspirations.

I'm sorry if I am a little complicated. I just want you to understand me. I'm not keeping quiet for the sake of one less argument. Let's argue if we have to. Let's disagree; let's free our thoughts and blunders. If I have only one shot at living my life and making it the best that I possibly can, I am going to do it no matter what and you better believe it will be free of any type of haunting.

Boo-Fearless,
Me.

Photo finish

How can one man be so endlessly disappointing?

Explain this to me:
Where is this love that you so profess because I can't see it, I can't touch it, I can't feel it? I can hear it, I hear some words but I can't do

anything with your easy words. What weight do they have? You don't know anything about love because you don't know anything about compromise. Love isn't simple. My heart isn't a diagram. You let your love for me drain out of you because it was difficult to keep up, and now you want to pretend that it's ok and you expect me to understand.

Deception is brutal and I'm not pretending otherwise. There is only one way to leave—I don't love you anymore, goodbye. Because that's the only reason why someone leaves. You don't leave someone you love.

Sounds real, eh? So did you.

Movie Trivia brought to you by the letter T-for TRUST. Trust that none of these words are mine. They sound real don't they? They sound heartfelt don't they?

So did you.

Hello reality, so nice of you to join me.

Inspired courtesy of "Closer,"
Me.

Movie must: [Closer]

Just a thought between the sewing madness
Just press play: [Led Zeppelin: Ramble On]

Dear love,

It's so amazing how thinking about you used to make me feel butterflies. When I think of you now my stomach feels like I just got off a roller coaster. As I stitch each picture, I remind myself just how unworthy you are.

And will always be,
Me.

Promises
Just press play: [Stars: Your X Lover Is Dead]

Because boys like to make promises but men never need to. All you have in this lifetime: your balls and your word.

"My father has never had to make me a promise because he's always kept his word. But then again my father has always been a man-" Audri Lopez

How much longer?
Just press play: [Kate Nash: Nicer Things]
(on repeat, why do we do this to ourselves?)

Dear horrible feeling,

Get the fuck out. You're driving me insane; mission accomplished. I'm not a deity. I'm hurt, I'm sad, I'm feeling the pricks of a million needles in my fucking veins; now leave. I'm desperately begging you. I've exhausted myself, no need to linger.

Me.

The early bird gets it

There is nothing like rising and shinning to inner peace. My meditation was enlightening this morning, despite the fact that I had to quiet my thoughts at least three times. It feels good to have insight again. How did I get to this place? It's so strange how bliss can carry us to uncharted territory, and in these places we somehow still feel safe even though we are surrounded by the somewhat unknown. The thing is that it's a temporary bliss and temporary safety. Sooner than later, at least for me, we begin to feel devoid of something and we start searching for our equanimity again. The truth is that it never left us; all along, it was there, way in the back. Our mind tells us that we should stay in the familiar and we should fear the unknown. But what is the familiar now?

We are one with our mind. Thoughts become things. If we truly want to be the change we see in the world we start with our temple first, our being.

On the 3rd day (well 2nd day for me) of my journey I am realizing that my body appreciates me a whole lot more than I have appreciated it. Forgive me my divine temple. I am one with myself, alone and steadfast.

Om-
Me.
Cheers to the future us**

Shot time: [Mamariña]

<u>Glass blower</u>

Dear boy,

I love the little glass blower:
She's so balsy and ride or die*ish* ... hats down to her today, for sure. She made me feel so much better. You have no idea. I always told you your words had weight. I tried to explain to you that when you say things to others

those things come with a responsibility and that very responsibility says a lot about you and the value you give your words.

I am VERY big on honoring my words. It is clear that you do not always honor yours. In any event, I, at the very least, hope that you love them enough to be able to eat them … especially the distasteful ones you texted me today. Those, love, you will be eating very soon. I'm truly sorry for not replying. Words that will later be eaten do not deserve to be acknowledged by me and therefore aren't. Oh, and also take extra time to think very carefully should you decide to dial my phone number. If it isn't for something of substance, which you can honor, don't waste your time calling me.
You only live once so feel free to go out there and do what makes you happy.
Enjoy eating your words for lunch and blowing glass for dinner or perhaps dessert. The little glass blower makes some pretty amazing stuff. Too bad she is inconsistent. I would like to personally order the "loved" nameplate for me because, apparently, I am.

[Insert Latin Phrase Here]
Lol,

Me.

Shot time: [Dirty Martini]

<u>Ab imo pectore</u>

Dear glass blower girl,

I have nothing against you or the Latin phrases that you have obviously taken the time to research. You can do whatever it is that you would like to entertain each other with. The fact that you are being told what I'm saying and you are voicing your comments about those things publicly tells me that you are extremely childish and disrespectful.

You don't know me, nor do you have the slightest clue of what is going on. You are nothing, a mere distraction as a result of a circumstance. Please do not be confused in this situation. You should know that you, too, can be the person in my shoes, and you would not like to be disrespected.

It would be smart not to be a participant of pointless banter. For clarification, you don't know me and you haven't a clue what has transpired. Nor is it any of your business, for that matter. Should anyone decide to fill you in, which is perfectly fine with me, and, definitely not under my control, you should learn to retain that information like an adult, not voice your meaningless opinions on a social network.

It is not my intention to disrespect you in any way. Again, I have nothing against you, nor do I care what you think. I don't care because you are not a factor in anything that is currently happening.

With all do respect, had you been a "true friend from the beginning" you wouldn't be an additive to the chaos. What you would be doing is defusing the situation but I understand that for lack of better judgment or simple incompetence you may not be capable of doing that. I have little, if any, tolerance for ignorant people … so don't fuck with me.

From the bottom of my heart,
Me.

Shot time: [Red Headed Slut] (I guess everyone's had one)
 Fake Fendis and other great knock offs

Just press play: [Kreayshawn: Gucci Gucci]

Dear love,

Remember when I used to tell you that I wasn't interested in relationships that resembled a fake Fendi? It wasn't because I was materialistic. I meant it figuratively. It wasn't because I wanted a Fendi. You know I have one (BTW, the zipper broke again). You promised you would fix it for me and there it is hanging in my closet with the rest of my feelings for you.

You should know that I'm upset now, mad and feeling resentment towards us. I was hurting pretty badly the first two days without you. But now I'm just plain disillusioned with this whole transition.

What I think is that I was an unfulfilled infatuation from your past. I came at a point when you were down and alone. I was the rebound from your last serious (well, not so serious) relationship. I'm happy to have been. I didn't hurt you. I didn't lead you on. I never lied to you. And last, but certainly not least, I loved you unconditionally. I still do.

Sure beats empty promises of forever, doesn't it? In fact, I think I was the perfect person to help you get safely back on the saddle. Don't you think? Come on, be honest. I just want you to know that in a few weeks, or perhaps days, you will realize what you did and what you have lost in this process, as will I. I love you, I really do. But I love myself more. I'm excited about my life and I would love for you to be a part of it. I have worked really hard for it and I know that I will reap the benefits and would love nothing more than to have you present every step of the way. I also want the fairytale. I want to be rescued, and I want to rescue that person right back, too. I am looking for someone supportive, emotionally charged, independent, secure and internally happy and fulfilled.

Do I think you could be that person? Yes. Do I think that you truthfully want to be? No—at least not for me you don't. It hurts to say that. But I own the feeling. I accept feeling that hurt. I understand that there is nothing that I can do if you have decided that I'm not the one, most importantly that I can't ever be no matter what. Ouch! I have always been clear with you about who I am. I thought we were on the same page when I opened up my tightly clenched fist and gave you my wounded heart to hold. I also clenched them right back tightly around my love for you.

In the words of the infamous Carrie Bradshaw: "I am someone who is looking for love, real love, ridiculous, inconvenient, consuming, can't live without each other love and I don't think that love is here."

It's not your fault. It's mine.
I don't have any intentions of sitting alone in any museums waiting for anyone. There is only one person that can make things happen for me in my life just the way I want them to, and that someone is me.

But thank you for the temporary blurriness and madness in this love. I meant that truthfully. It was nice to dance with desire and be magically transported to a life of happily ever after. As much as I hate to admit it, I enjoyed being the "in-love", dumbfounded schoolgirl again. It was great to know that I didn't have to worry, to feel that I *needed* you when I thought this was, indeed, real love.

But, reality is also nice because it is real. Everything isn't what it seems to be. There will always be knock-offs. But when it comes to relationships, I'm not the girl that is looking for a good imitation of the real thing.

There is only one Fendi.
Me.
Cheers**

Sleepless...

Tired of elevated hopes and failed expectations...

Rocky roads
Just press play: [The Source ft. Candie Station: You've Got The Love]

Dear love,

We begin to live when we can live outside ourselves. Our problems will not be solved using the same kind of thinking that created them. A paradigm shift must occur.
Chameleon,
Me.

Vicarious occasions

Just press play: [Alanis Morissette: Not The Doctor]

Dear love,

This may read a bit distilled and sterile. I'm sorry for that, but you've exhausted me.

Demand: –verb (used with object)
1. To ask for with proper authority; claim as a right.

I want to take the time to explain to you how I feel about demands. Demands have no place and simply will not be quartered by me. I am giving you the benefit of the doubt in hopes that you will read this carefully without ripping it apart trying to find out what I mean when I use certain words or phrases. It is clear and should not be misinterpreted.

Some things just are and we get to choose if we agree with what and how they "are". It's a two-part thing, you see. There is always a compromise involved. I have come this far and it wasn't because I was being demanded of or insulted in any way.

I won't sugarcoat anything for anyone but I am still very careful not to hurt the ones I love, because I understand that not everyone thinks and acts like me. In reality, this is no reflection upon you. It is my choice and the manner in which I choose to do things in my life—not yours.

(You shouldn't take offense or read into anything I write too much. It is what it is, plain and simple.)

Insult: –verb (used with object)
1. To treat or speak to insolently or with contemptuous rudeness; affront.
2. To affect as an affront; offend or demean.

As human beings, we owe one another esteem or a sense of worth for personal qualities or abilities. We don't get to freely go about bad mouthing others and irresponsibly blurting careless opinions that should clearly be thought out way before thought exits mouth.

I am trying to clean up my life one way or the other and I do not want errant thoughts provoking haphazard words and decisions fueled by thoughts and not necessarily

emotions. What are you doing with your life and the way you live it?
(Take a moment to think about this deeply.)

I'm not sure that there can ever be a cooling off period between us. It's not healthy for you to be the way you are, never mind me in that scenario.

(Don't read into this. Just simply take a step back and think about your thoughts.)

There has never been a time where things have lingered between us. Things have been crystal clear since day one. I place the blame totally on myself, perhaps for not being clear enough, though I'm not sure what else I could have said or done. I feel that it wouldn't be thorough enough for you regardless. Again, never mind me in that scenario.
I also placed the burden upon you to respect me. I say burden because I realize that respect is not something that you often practice or implement in your life on a daily basis.
 (Perhaps this is why you act how you do)

I don't want there to be any confusion in the future. Everyone that I choose to have in my life will respect me. Like I said, we have a choice. That is what I choose. When I feel disrespected, I retract. I hope you realize sooner than later that you are alone in this large and unforgiving world. We all are. We are lucky to have ourselves to take refuge in. We have our thoughts, our actions, and our feelings. We have our minds, too. Nonetheless, we are obligated to learn how to make it and that will require other human beings (like ourselves) since we do not occupy the planet alone. In that process there will be times where we are misunderstood and we have to cope and try to understand the others that we choose to have in our lives.

(That is called compromise.)

That doesn't mean that anyone is required to understand us. It means that we try to learn. We don't get to do as we please with those that we may not understand. We don't get to bad mouth them and put them down when misunderstandings occur. At that point, we combine compromise and respect and this is how we build relationships.

(Please read this paragraph several times— perhaps you should print it and have it with you always)

Take this, as you will need to in order to understand me. I have made a decision, one that you will not be able to reconcile. Realize that nothing can ever come out of this because I have a drawn a well-defined line and I can now move forward from there. You, on the other hand, have no lines or boundaries. Perhaps that is why it is so easy for you to cross others disrespectfully. They say you should start at the beginning, but where is the beginning? You can draw your line and start to move forward whenever you want, you choose. But you have to choose, you have to create that starting point and only then will you begin to move forward.

"An apple a day keeps the doctor away." Too bad you don't like apples.

Either way, I'm not the doctor,
Me.
 Piercing the Veil: Ode to The Ketalar
Just press play: [Pierce the Veil: Caraphernelia]

"When something brings you down, the best thing to do is to cut it out completely, from the very source; from the root." –Vic Fuentes

This is what I'm going to do before I let it build up anymore and hurt me more over time, if that is even possible. I'm piercing the veil in your honor tonight. Because I realize that I've become so numb and robotic and that is not I. This weight is going to lift completely out of me; not another day of viciously overthinking this nonsense in spite of my anguish. I've been so hard on "me" and what for, undeserving selfish you? I'm tired of wondering what I did. I did nothing. It isn't my fault that your words are empty and weightless. I can't ever fix that because I'm not the doctor. Find refuge in your emptiness. Find love in your lies. Find hope in your banter. But for the love of anything you ever believed in, find yourself.

Spaceship Star has landed. So what does this mean? I'll tell you in another lifetime when we are both cats.
Hopelessly devoted to,
Me.
(Something you can't ever be ... How sad for you)

Grow up
Just press play: [Ray Lamontagne: Trouble]

I'm over it. When you are ready to understand yourself and the way you live your life you come find me. I've tried so many times to explain to you that we only have one chance to make it right and you just don't get it. You have this one opportunity to right your wrongs and go out there and make it happen but you choose not to.

You say you love me. Well... prove it! Stand up for this love you say you feel so deeply. You know what I think? I think your full of it. I think you're a poor excuse for a wannabe hopeless romantic that wants to live that happily ever after but doesn't want to fight for it.

I see a childish little boy stuck in this manly body, still throwing tantrums and not understanding simple common sense. So, feel free to sit in timeout until you get it. You need help. You have ghosts from your past haunting your present. I already dealt with mine. I don't have the energy to deal with yours, especially not on a daily basis. So, yes, I am walking away. I can be your friend and nothing else. Not because I don't want to be in a relationship with you but because time and time again you prove to me that you are incapable of being in one.

Time is not standing still for you or anyone for that matter. You're going to lose me, and in doing so, you're going to lose the one woman who has ever genuinely cared about you without a hidden agenda.

So be my guest, fuck this up. Trust me, I expect you to fail at loving me and at making this happen. Because how can I not expect it when it is what you have done every other time?

Walking away my friend.
Me.

That awkward moment when....
Just press play: [Manchester Orchestra: Apprehension]

You wake up from a dream you're having about someone you're in love with and you're relieved it isn't real, and it isn't, because if anything bad happened to them it's because you're so paranoid that you're back in the vicious cycle.

Love to love you from far away,
Me.

Would've, Could've, Should've
Just press play: [Johann Nepomuk Hummel: Piano Concerto in A minor, Op.85]

You could be brilliant, but you're a coward.

Grin,
Me.

Chronic Indecision
Just press play: [Envy On The Coast: Starving Your Friends]

The worst part is that after everything, I just think you didn't love me enough to say "Fuck you past, I'm not going to let you get the best of me," and for those reasons, I believe you are in love with your ex who fucked you over, wished you to fail every day, and probably still does.

That is the irony of life. We take chances, we fall in love and at the end of the day if we are

left empty and heartbroken we can count on the mind to say the infamous words "I told you so." -
The consolation prize, then, is: We all float on.

Modest,
Me.

<u>Another beautiful sunrise, in your perfectly beautiful life.</u>

I'm so happy that you're moving on in your pretend perfection where you are perfect, where your past is not a factor, where you will someday be living in Gables by the Sea, with your perfect housewife, your perfect Fila Brasileiro, your perfect boat, car and bank account. Perfectly imperfect and isn't that what we all are?

I'm so proud of you for forgetting,
Me

<u>Why</u>
Just press play: [Zero 7: Waiting Game]

Why do you insist on hurting the people who actually care about you? You're so shady. I'm expecting the worst from you, but it is only through this time of suffering that I realize how strong I truly am inside. I'm eternally grateful. Thank you for forcing me to look forward no matter how much I need or want to look back.

I can't,
Me.

Time for me to fly...
Just press play: [REO Speedwagon: Time For Me To Fly]

When you love someone, you open yourself up to suffering, and that's the sad truth. Maybe they'll break your heart, or maybe you'll break their heart and never be able to look at yourself in the same way. Those are the risks, and that's the burden. Like wings, they have weight. We feel the weight on our backs but they are the burden that lifts us up and allow us to fly.

Logic
Just press play: [Envy On The Coast: Made Of Stone]

I fought for us. I fought with everything I had to be with you. Hell, I even fought with myself, because everyone, including my better judgment, was telling me that I was going to get my heart broken. But, I took a chance with you anyway. I put my heart and my pride on the line—and, in the end, my judgment won.

Forgive and Forget
Just press play: [Envy On The Coast: Lapse]

I can never forgive you or forget you. So either way I'm dammed. I try to push you out of my mind but I can't. Perhaps because I don't understand how you can be so selfish and emotionally unattached. I miss you so much but I'd rather miss you and never see or hear from you again than allow you back into my life. What you've done to me, I will never forgive or forget.

Unforgiving,
Me.

Mind over Matter
Just press play: [Beck: Everybody's Gotta Learn Sometime]

It's been almost two months. I haven't felt this much animosity towards someone in my entire life. This has affected me in so many ways, creatively especially.

It's surprisingly difficult for me to do things since you always find your way into my mind. I still can picture the rose you drew for me, and how you thought you could have done better, though it was beautiful.

I miss you terribly. I have your scars now but still … I miss you.

I miss the way you got mad at me when our plans didn't go through the way you hoped. I miss your phone calls and crazy text messages.
I don't know why. I shouldn't because you hurt me and you mistreated me, unknowingly, I guess, but that doesn't excuse your madness, nor does it make the soreness in my insides go away.

I miss our passion; though I am convinced it was all false pretense on your part. I miss the way you reassured me that you loved me and cared about me, and how I never doubted you. I never wanted to tell you that I was the jealous type, but I always was. I never thought you could be my type, maybe that's why.

Now, I think back about how you said, "you weren't the one for me," and I wish I could tell you to your face how right you were. I don't regret the things I'm not proud of doing because I realize that the past is set in stone, and, I know "should have" doesn't exist, but I really wish it did exist with you.

You hurt me but I also hurt myself and I continue to hurt myself trying to repress my feelings to get over you and it's working. I was always broken.

In a way, I'm glad this happened to me because for the first time in my life, I truly grasp the concept of love everyday. Some days are harder than others but on most days I remind myself how I wanted to lose hope. I wanted to lose hope because I wanted to protect my feelings and know that I've lost all hope. My feelings are more hurt than I ever thought possible and I am becoming a stronger person as a result of this.

You taught me that I needed to be vulnerable sometimes. You also taught me that people don't change and they also aren't always genuine. You taught me that being bare means to really expose your insides and nothing could protect those. You taught me that being guarded means not ever trusting anyone no matter who they were. You taught me to doubt love. You told me so many times that you weren't good for me and I never got the chance to thank you.

You've made me so jaded and I know that somehow makes you happy. I know that reading this also makes you happy. You told me once, "When you write about me, good or bad, it makes me happy because it's ME you are writing about."
Every night I go to bed alone, wondering, waiting, hoping, praying, wanting, needing, crying, tossing and turning. What for? You.

And you are so not worth what I'm going through. You're a sleepwalker. Day in and day out you live your life like its owed to you, not understanding that it isn't. You let your past get the best of us and I just want you to explain one thing to me: If you loved me, if you were so sure that I was the one then how could you let me walk away? How could you forget us?

I hate you for pretending to love me.
I hate you for pretending that you would do anything for us.
I hate you for forgetting to specify it was only if things were the way you wanted them to be that we would make it.
I hate you for telling me that you wanted to be with me forever.
I hate you for giving me failed hopes.
I hate you for giving me false and elevated expectations.
I hate you for your empty promises.
I hate you for your lies.
I hate you.
Love to hate you,
Me.

You and Her

Today I found out you have a new girlfriend. I hope you are happy.
And, that they lived happily ever after. Good for you!

iLyfe<3
Me.

Life.

Just press play: [Mumford And Sons: Awake My Soul]

Whenever possible, life should be a pattern of experiences to savor, not to endure.

<u>With my honey to the moon...</u>
Just press play: [La Dispute: Such Small Hands]

I dreamed of us last night.
In a series of craziness, much like our relationship, I dreamed that we were at a happy hour and you started kissing me. I was freaking out, of course. We left together and you took me to your house, forgetting that you were now married. When we got to your neighborhood you realized that you no longer lived there but you pointed at your new house with her.

In the dream, I was really nervous and anxious and I really didn't care how any of this would end, much less how it would make her feel. I decide to follow your lead and we walked inside your new house. Your brother was waiting for you sitting on the couch and he was pretty upset that you were with me. We walked in and she said hello to the both of us not knowing who I was exactly.

She was preparing to host some type of gathering for some guests (who arrived later) while I was waiting for you to shower and get ready to leave with me. At this point, there was really no turning back. I'm super happy just knowing that you are leaving with me. I feel that I have won.

When the guests arrive, they know me, and, overwhelmed with excitement, they call my name. This obviously blows my cover. She figures out who I am and flips her lid. You just look at her and tell her you are sorry. Next thing I know the three of us are at an office annulling your marriage.

She was so sad. The look of failure overcame her splendor. I was laughing and we were hugging and having a great time. Suddenly, it dawned on me—I stopped for a second and looked at you and thought about our tumultuous past, and, then, I thought to myself: "Now what am I going to do? I don't love him; I don't want to be with him. Even after all this I am still bittersweet."

Just then I realized I was dreaming and I felt

so relieved; funny how the mind works.

Loving the Orchids in the Banana Republic,
Me.

Survey Says: Wild Card
Just press play: [Bjork: Unravel]

At the end of the day, what it comes down to
is a photo finish and there is never ever a dull
moment, infamous shoulder tap, wildcard …
and I wouldn't have it any other way.
Staying passionate,
Me.

Postcards (Ode to Sarah Kay)
Just press play: [Sarah Kay: Postcards]

I used to watch Sarah Kay's slam poetry
performance of "Postcards" on YouTube and
wonder how she felt. Now, *I'm* the girl who
still writes you because she doesn't know how
not to.
Valentine's Day: Will you be mine?
Just press play: [Cranberries: Just My
Imagination]

Sometimes, the thrill is in the chase. If you
genuinely are in love you will go through

extreme measures to prove your love and to teach a lesson. And, if you aren't, well, then you don't have to do anything. Here is the thing, though. Women are generally waiting to be rescued and men are generally scared.

What sucks about this arrangement is that too often we mistake a lot of things for love like perhaps the "idea" of love and being loved and we get confused about what love actually is and what it feels like. By that time we are in our 30s and going through some sort of midlife crises, we then say to ourselves: "Is this love or is this a midlife crises?
Hence, there we are … right were we started.

Woman: I want the fairy tale.
Man: I am not Edward Lewis.

We really want to know what it is like to be rescued. But how do we separate genuine from douchebag? It's a difficult task, and, especially hard on holidays; holidays such as Valentine's Day, where it's a douche-eat-douche world.

So, in ode to all the douches—both women and men—you will not be mine. But, hey, look at the bright side; you can still be each others.

* Dedicated to my favorite Leo.

Forever the fairytale,
Me.

<u>#Him</u>
Just press play: [She Wants Revenge: Tear You Apart]
This *is* for you.

You are too hard on yourself. Life does not come with an instruction manual. So, what if you are [insert your age here] years old? This does not mean your life is over. In the same vein, what if you made some bad decisions in the past. This is not it. This vortex that you claim to be in is self-created. So get out!

If you want it, then get it. Why not? Everyone else does it. So why shouldn't you be able to? The only thing stopping you is yourself and your fear of the unfamiliar for the safety and comfort of what is known. You'd rather stay unhappy in the familiar, than risking it, anything, for the unknown, even if it means being happy. CRAZY!

You have so much going for you that you don't see. You are smart, sexy, funny, (sometimes, lol) quirky, laid back and young. I don't understand what it is that is holding you back, other than your fear?

People fail. Henry Ford didn't build Ford Motors on the first try. In fact, he failed countless times before the automobile juggernaut was established. Not everyone is Bill Gates, either. But he failed a plenty, too. It isn't that hard to figure out, though.

You try until you are happy and you don't give up. It isn't going to be easy. On the contrary, it's probably going to be very hard. But then again, the easy choices in life are never the right ones.

Release yourself form the eternal glorified roommate chokehold.

Rome,
Me.

Swift feet on a muddy path
Just press play: [John Lennon: Jealous Guy]

Cheaters:
Fuck you, for cheating on me.
Fuck you for reducing me to one word. This isn't a card game. And who invented the word cheater, anyway? Perhaps, someone who thought liar and devastator were way too harsh is who invented it. That was probably the same person who wasn't consistent enough to give their feelings any emotional weight. Fuck you! This isn't about making up a word in a game of scrabble. These are lives; lives that you go and break—and you, are so much worse then a cheater. You killed something and you killed it when it wasn't looking … gutless.

Committed,
Me.

High Expectations
Just press play: [Death Cab for Cutie: Dream Scream]

After having numerous conversations about love and relationships with a lot of different people I realize that a lot of us have had the same experience on more than one occasion. We have had a serious infatuation. We have been in love with the idea of love.

Infatuation: The state of being completely carried away by unreasoned passion; an addictive adoration; an unusual love where one is inspired with an intense but short-lived admiration for someone.

A concept; something imagined. So we fall in love with the idea of a man. If you are like me you fall in love with the highest potential of that idea then you wait perpetually for him to ascend into his awesomeness. During this waiting game you build his ego and turn him into this massive lion of a man when in reality he still just a baby kitten. You watch him as he becomes a little more your "greatest version" of him everyday. You watch him go through trials and tribulations, peeks and valleys. And then one day he reaches "his" greatness and you are finally disappointed.

Your expectation of awesomeness may be too high. Sometimes the end result of his ascending and your expectations never quite measure up.

After having numerous conversations about love and relationships with a lot of different people I realize that a lot of us have had the same experience on more than one occasion.

We are simply in love with the "idea" of love.

Love to love,
Me.

<u>Seek to express</u>
Just press play: [Andrew Bird: Anonimal]

Sometimes I feel a little lost. But I prefer
being lost than having to depend on anyone
else to get me to where I need to be. That is
the thing about being alone; good, bad or in
between, it is always if nothing else, my own.

<u>To Ms. from Mrs.</u>
Just press play: [The Weepies: World Spins
Madly On]

I broke up with the China today.
I set it free for someone else to have his or her
way with it.
I wrapped the drinking glasses in old
newspaper and I watched the forks and knives
argue about reality and make pretend.
I counted the teacups and plates we were
getting rid of along with the pots and pans and
the oven gloves.

All the old doilies and kitchen rags, I just threw them in some paper bag named What if.

As for yesterday's wine glasses, those I kept. I plan on breaking them into a new tomorrow with lots of hope and little, if any, sorrow.

I contemplated the day we bought most things, old coffee mugs and tethered vases, and wondered about and within. I'm not sure how to hold together what the mind replaces and all the empty spaces inside the cabinets and shelves where memories still hide … the heart erases.

All the scents and smells and the seasons of sad days, old floury trails and cake mixes, sugary betrayals and quick fixes.

Some things I kept but most I threw out. Admittedly, it was hard to let go of what once fit so nicely … would've, could've, should've … but not quite.

I swept up the dust of what used to be the front door watching the pieces of doubt and regret float around less and more.

The little bird inside me is wondering what will be and what we had … both scared and sad … a little empty in my bitter-sweetness, to Ms. from Mrs.

The Law- La La La
Just press play: [Goyte: Someone I Use To Know]

So, this is where we are. After a series of almost interactions, we have been reduced to a text or a call every so often. It is sad how we have slowly faded. You are still my muse. It is those times when my creativity is nonexistent that I hear your voice the clearest; kind of reminds me of Bella when she purposely does careless things to see Edward. I know that is a pretty cliché comparison. And, although to me, you are a tall, brilliant poem, we both know you are everything but shiny. If anything you are dull and dark but there is a strange beauty in your darkness. As strange as it may seem, you are still very present in my work, and, more importantly, even more present in my heart.

What a stupid,
Me.

<u>Man appoints and God disappoints</u>
Just press play: [Carly Simon: You're so Vain]

So, today you told me that women throw themselves at you and that you think that is pathetic. You also told me you like women that are confident, such as your ex-wife. Wow! That is such a vain observation. Then again, you're so vain; you probably think this entry is about you. I'm not at all surprised that your newly found spiritual inspiration has brought you full circle with your "self". I understand that and I commend you for your 180-degree about-face. In the meantime, you have managed to successfully make me understand that the pedestal I have had you on for the past 6 years is imaginary. Another failed attempt at me waiting for you to ascend into your self proclaimed greatness.

It saddens me so deeply to let go of my idea of us. That's just it, it's "my" idea. It is also an unrealistic expectation of a lingering "what if". I think you are great. I love so many things about you. But what I don't love about you is that you hurt me. You've hurt me several times. I'm sure it was unintentional, but, still, you hurt me. Perhaps that makes me needy and insecure but the truth is that just makes you insensitive and you shouldn't be, because a man of your caliber should be sensitive to a woman's emotions, especially a woman such as me.

Despite the ups and downs of our friendship I have always been there for you, unconditionally. Even now, I am still here. I am always here. If the time should ever come where you are in a bind and in need of anything you well know that I will drop everything and come to your rescue. But that doesn't mean that you can belittle my feelings. If this is how I feel, I imagine a lot of other women must feel the same.
So when you say you are "tired of women throwing themselves at you" it makes you shallow. You should be flattered that women flock to your presence. You should also see it as an opportunity to choose whom you want to be with. You aren't a prize. "Judge not, lest you be judged"

You create this illusion. You make everything great. You keep women hanging on to your last call, your last text and your last acronym. You leave them on the edge of the oddly pointed knife and when you lose interest you claim that they are throwing themselves at you. You have issues saying no gracefully. The truth is, you are careless and facing the truth—that you have lost interest—is tough. Your intentions are not to hurt them but that is exactly what you do by avoiding the evident. I know, and the reason why I know is because you did it to me.

Redeemed,
Me.

<u>Big Love- Logistics</u>
Just press play: [Edward Sharpe and The Magnetic Zeros: Home]

For what it's worth, polygamy is both illegal and not allowed by the church at this point, and, of course, I get that. That said, it is still considered an eternal principle, and I personally suspect it may be reinstated at some point (thanks to you). Let's just say that I consider it within the realm of possibility that some of us may eventually be asked to live the principle … and I'll admit I do not think I could manage doing so.

So, in a spur of romantic bliss you told me you were leaving your old ways behind you and you wanted to know if I would be yours. That statement made me panic a little. I wasn't sure what you meant, and since your intentions have never been clear, I can't say I took you seriously. Yesterday, you told me: "Your predictions were correct I have met my Scorpio," and I'm happy for you. I should take this time to tell you that I highly admire your intelligence. I think you have what it takes to be a great father. But I don't think you have what it takes to be a great husband, although you may at some point.

We had our share of great times and I want you to know that as a result of me clearing my path of unnecessary complications you didn't make the cut. But it isn't because I don't love and care for you. It is because I am disappointed that you underestimated me. Now you stand corrected. I am not like the rest of your girl"friends" who: wake up in the morning feeling like P-Diddy, nor am I impressed by your degrees or the fact that you still want to go to law school. Your large words and mathematical equations about love and the justifications of emotional stress mean nothing to me.

Maybe I am selfish, childish, immature, irrational, illogical, emotional, sensitive, imbalanced, prude, inexperienced, argumentative, ball-busting and un-matrixy, but that is the beauty of life.

I am me, something they'll never be. And, for what it's worth, it was pretty and shiny and maybe they would have fallen to your feet in polygamous bliss. As for me, I can't even find it.

A girl's best friend,
Me.

Everything will be different tomorrow...
Just press play: [Pearl Jam: Elderly Woman Behind The Counter In A Small Town]
Just press play: [The Cranberries: Linger]

Dear love,

What I've learned thus far …
Last night, I dreamt with an old cassette deck. In the dream, I kept on playing "Linger" by the Cranberries over and over again. It was a

Fuji cassette and in red faded ink it said "Elderly Women Behind the Counter in a Small Town." I couldn't help but wonder why it said that on the outside and what was actually on it was "Linger." I didn't understand the message within the message and I will leave it up to you to decipher. But I will tell you this: The mind is vast.

Vast: –adjective
1. Of very great area or extent; immense; like the ocean the sky and outer space.

I don't think we understand its power. I think that we underestimate what we can do with our minds. I don't think we really understand when we so often read things like "thoughts become things" because when they really do, we actually are left dumbfounded and wondering what happened. If only we would carefully listen to the voice of reasoning. If only we would concentrate in the things that we truly want to accomplish, the things that make us blissfully happy, and the things that we are meant to be doing. Ahh, but that is all too easy. So, what do we do? We choose to focus on the things that we don't want to experience because we are so afraid of going through the pain. But, what ends up happening?

After carefully thinking about my dream last night, searching the lyrics several times and trying to figure out the message, I realize that, I, too, was afraid. I was so afraid of losing you that in the process I lost myself. But inadvertently something great has come out of the madness. Something larger than me, something larger than us, something larger than I ever imagined my pain could ever be.

I can listen to our favorite song a million times and go over the same scenario in my mind time and time again but eventually hearts and thoughts they fade ... fade away. I've decided to remove all of my love letter posts from this blog after this, my 100th post this year, and write a book. You know I'm such a fool for you ...

Not at all, **
Me.

"This is what I needed to jolt me back to reality." -SATC

Just press play: [The Verve: Bittersweet Symphony]

So what does this all mean?

Where are they now and what is next?
Well,

The Fulfiller has moved on, and moved out. We are still close and we will always be family.

The Visionary is living his life in the now as always. I had given our moment an expiration date, count down to "fun and me" 38 on the 28th. But after our last fall out I realize that "fun and free" is all we will ever be, and, although we are no longer "Facebook friends", he is still my "person" despite all the non-sense we tell each other.

The Thinker is doing well and thinking logically. The last time we spoke his ex had called him back with some interesting news about the possibility of her first born being his.

The Executive, my dear Libra, is happy with his counterpart—not a Gemini, and not me.

<u>The Protector,</u> well I could go on and on forever about this, but I won't bore you with disappointment. I'm assuming he is doing just fine. As of today, I haven't spoken to him in three months and I don't plan on speaking to him ever again. I, however, hear a rumor that some wedding bells were ringing!

As for me, I'm single and happily embracing the now; living in Miami, taking lots of pictures, working on "The Girlfriend Diaries" and searching for Marc (a fictional character of a dwindling breed that I have created. In my mind he is *still* perfect.)
Marc: Love Ignited.

The Boy "friend" Diaries Musical Playlist by entry:

1. <u>Almost Interactions</u>: 10,000 Maniacs - Circle Dream
2. <u>Distance and Time:</u> Dashboard Confessionals - Vindicated
3. <u>Past or present, what shall it be?</u> Righteous Brothers - Unchained Melody
4. <u>The truth shall settle:</u> Peter Gabriel - In Your Eyes
5. <u>Will it ever end?</u>: Limp Bizkit - My Way
6. <u>Quality reality TV = my life</u>: DJ Nancy Starr - Ego Trip 42
7. <u>Daydreaming and dumbfounded</u>: The Killers - Leave The Bourbon On The Shelf
8. <u>And the academy award goes to:</u> Lykke Li - Little Bit
9. <u>The Pussy Chase:</u> Mickey Avalon - My Dick
10. <u>Observing</u>: The Soup Dragons - I'm Free
11. <u>Vie:</u> Coldplay - The Scientist
12. <u>The finer things:</u> Kate Nash - I Hate Seagulls
13. <u>Vent:</u> John Mayer - Say
14. <u>Happy and full</u>: Mazzy Starr - Fade Into You

15. <u>All roads lead to love:</u> Sting - Shape Of My Heart
16. <u>Lost in London:</u> Lykke Li - Time Flies
17. <u>More than one side:</u> Neon Trees - Animal
18. <u>Plebian:</u> Lykke Li - Possibility
19. <u>The difference between disaster and deliverance is life:</u> Postal Service - Such Great Heights
20. <u>Pyrrhic-victory:</u> Third Eye Blind - How's It Gonna Be
21. <u>Post Pangaea – My rendition of a 15<u>th</u> century love letter:</u> Debussy - Clair De Lune
22. <u>Time:</u> Paolo Nutini - Last Request
23. <u>Wild card:</u> Antonio Carlos Jobim - Girl From Ipanema
24. <u>Diaphanously, imprisoned:</u> Kaoma - Lambada
25. <u>Perhaps:</u> Boz Scaggs - Look What You've Done
26. <u>The secret weapon:</u> Jay-Z-Brush - Your Shoulders Off
27. <u>Lead me, love me:</u> Foreigner - I Want To Know What Love Is
28. <u>Make a mess of my insides; I want to feel disoriented in this lust:</u> The Temper Trap - Sweet Disposition

29. <u>It's a bird, it's a plane, it's:</u> Ludacris - Move Bitch
30. <u>Blah, blah, blah- or words:</u> Deelight - Groove Is In The Heart
31. <u>What dreams may come:</u> This will destroy you - The World is Our ____
32. <u>Taming the beast:</u> Limp Bizkit - Break Stuff
33. <u>The love we deserve:</u> Gregory And The Hawk - Boats And Birds
34. <u>Don't let it get the best of you:</u> The Shins - Caring Is Creepy
35. <u>Sweet, sweet love:</u> Adele - Rolling In The Deep
36. <u>WHAT IS IT THAT YOU WANT FROM ME?:</u> Lady Gaga -Speechless
37. <u>A conversation of mind and heart:</u> Imogen Heap - Hide And Seek
38. <u>Buh-bye:</u> Two Door Cinema Club - Something Good Can Work
39. <u>Hialeah Helan vs NYC Tolle:</u> Frank Sinatra - NY, NY
40. <u>Insides and outsides:</u> Phoenix - Lisztomania
41. <u>Not understanding:</u> Amy Winehouse - Back To Black
42. <u>Just a thought between the sewing madness:</u> Led Zeppelin - Ramble On
43. <u>Promises:</u> Stars - Your X Lover Is Dead

44. <u>How much longer:</u> Kate Nash - Nicest Things
45. <u>Fake Fendis and other great knock offs:</u> Kreayshawn - Gucci Gucci
46. <u>Rocky roads:</u> The Source ft. Candie Station - You've Got The Love
47. <u>Vicarious occasions:</u> Alanis Morissette - Not The Doctor (Acoustic)
48. <u>Piercing the Veil Ode to The Ketalar:</u> Pierce the Veil - Caraphernelia
49. <u>Grow up:</u> Ray Lamontagne - Trouble
50. <u>That Awkward moment when:</u> Manchester Orchestra - Apprehension
51. <u>Could've, would've, should've:</u> Johann Nepomok - Piano Concerto in A minor, Op 85
52. <u>Chronic indecision:</u> Envy On The Coast - Starving Your Friends
53. <u>Why:</u> Zero7 - Waiting Game
54. <u>Time for me to fly:</u> REO Speedwagon - Time For Me To Fly
55. <u>Logic:</u> Envy On The Coast - Made of Stone
56. <u>Forgive and Forget:</u> Envy On The Coast - Lapse
57. <u>Mind Over Matter:</u> Beck - Everybody's Gotta Learn Sometime
58. <u>With My Honey To The Moon:</u> La Dispute - Such Small Hands

59. <u>Survey Says(WildCard):</u> Bjork - Unravel
60. <u>Postcards (Ode to Sarah Kay):</u> Sarah Kay - Postcards
61. <u>Valentine's Day (Will you be mine?):</u> Cranberries - Just My Imagination
62. <u>#Him:</u> She Wants Revenge - Tear You Apart
63. <u>Swift feet on muddy Path:</u> John Lennon - Jealous Guy
64. <u>High expectations:</u> Death Cab For Cutie - Dram Scream
65. <u>Seek to express:</u> Andrew Bird - Anonimal
66. <u>To Ms. from Mrs.:</u> The Weepies - World Spins Madly On
67. <u>The Law (La, La, La):</u> Goyte - Someone I Use To Know
68. <u>Man Appoints, God Disappoints:</u> Carly Simon - You're So Vain
69. <u>Big Lov (Logistics):</u> Edward Sharpe and The Magnetic Zeros - Home
70. <u>Everything will be different tomorrow:</u> Pearl Jam - Elderly Woman Behind The Counter In A Small Town/Cranberries - Linger
71. <u>"This is what I needed to jolt me back to reality." –SATC:</u> The Verve - Bittersweet Symphony

www.ingramcontent.com/pod-product-compliance
Lightning Source LLC
Chambersburg PA
CBHW051927240626
47153CB00004B/1400